Bird-footed Dinosaurs

Robin Birch

CHELSEA CLUBHOUSE
An Imprint of Chelsea House Publishers

Chelsea Clubhouse books are available at special discounts when purchased in bulk quantities for businesses, associations, institutions, or sales promotions. Please call our Special Sales Department in New York at (212) 967-8800 or (800) 322-8755.

You can find Chelsea Clubhouse on the World Wide Web at: http://www.chelseahouse.com

First published in 2002 by
MACMILLAN EDUCATION AUSTRALIA PTY LTD
15–19 Claremont Street, South Yarra, 3141

Visit our Web site at www.macmillan.com.au or go directly to www.macmillanlibrary.com.au

Associated companies and representatives throughout the world.

Copyright © Robin Birch 2009; 2002

Library of Congress Cataloging-in-Publication Data
Birch, Robin.
  Bird-footed dinosaurs / by Robin Birch.
    p. cm. — (Dinosaur world)
  Summary: Describes the appearance, eating habits, and habitat of bird-footed dinosaurs, including Iguanodon, Hypsilophodon, Maiasaura, Parasaurolophus, and Corythosaurus.
  Includes index.
  ISBN 978-1-60413-405-6
  1. Ornithischia—Juvenile literature. [1. Ornithischians. 2. Dinosaurs.] I. Title. II.Series.
  QE862.O65 B57 2009
  567.914—dc21

                                        2008000845

Edited by Angelique Campbell-Muir
Illustrations by Nina Sanadze
Page layout by Nina Sanadze

Printed in the United States of America

Acknowledgements
Department of Library Services, American Museum of Natural History (neg. no. PK51), p. 9; Auscape/ James L. Amos & Peter Arnold, p. 5, Auscape/Parer & Parer-Cook, p. 13; © The Natural History Museum, London, pp. 8 (bottom), 12, 16; Getty Images/Photodisc, p. 24; Royal Tyrrell Museum of Palaeontology/ Alberta Community Development, pp. 8 (top), 29.

While every care has been taken to trace and acknowledge copyright, the publisher tenders their apologies for any accidental infringement where copyright has proved untraceable.

Contents

Glossary words
When a word is printed in
bold, you can look up its
meaning in the Glossary
on page 31.

Dinosaurs

Dinosaurs lived and died millions of years ago.

There were many different kinds of dinosaurs.

After dinosaurs died, their bones sometimes became buried. We know what dinosaurs were like because scientists have dug up and studied their bones.

This scientist is scraping rock away from dinosaur bones.

Bird Feet

Some dinosaurs ate animals and others ate plants. Some of the plant-eating dinosaurs had feet like birds' feet. These dinosaurs had three toes on each back foot.

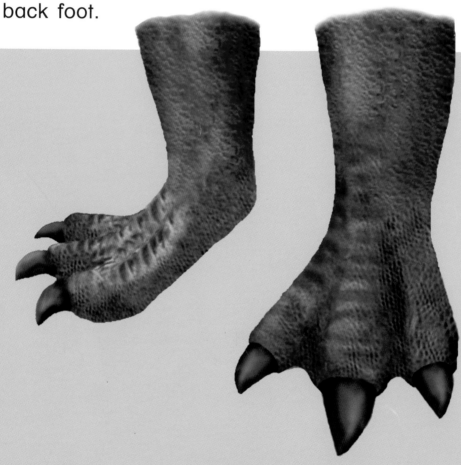

Bird-footed dinosaurs had claws on their toes.

Bird-footed dinosaurs probably walked on both their arms and legs. But they probably ran fastest on just their legs.

walking

running

Bird-footed dinosaurs used only their legs to run.

The plant-eating, bird-footed dinosaurs had hard beaks. Usually they did not have teeth in their beaks. Instead, these dinosaurs had sharp teeth farther back in their cheeks. It is hard to see these teeth in their **skulls**.

Bird-footed dinosaurs had hard beaks.

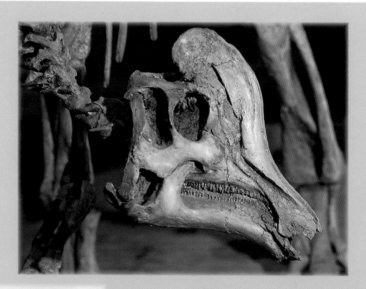

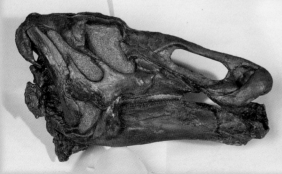

Bird-footed dinosaurs had no teeth in their beaks.

Bird-footed dinosaurs laid eggs, as all other dinosaurs did. Some eggs did not hatch. After many years, they turned into rock. The rock eggs are a type of **fossil**.

These dinosaur-egg fossils are made of rock.

Iguanodon

(ih-GWAN-uh-don)

Iguanodon was a big, heavy dinosaur. It had strong back feet with three toes on each foot. It also had a long, **stiff** tail.

long stiff tail

Iguanodon was a big dinosaur with strong feet.

10

Instead of thumbs on its front hands, Iguanodon had strong, sharp spikes made of bone. Iguanodon may have used these spikes to fight other dinosaurs if it was attacked.

sharp spike for thumb

Iguanodon probably bit off ferns and other low plants with its beak. Then it chewed them with its cheek teeth.

sharp tooth edge

sharp tooth edge

Iguanodon teeth had sharp edges for slicing tough leaves.

Iguanodons lived in large groups called herds. The **herds** usually roamed flat lands near rivers in search of food. Today, many animals live in herds.

Many animals live in herds, just as dinosaurs used to.

Hypsilophodon

(hip-sil-OFF-o-don)

Hypsilophodon was a small, slim dinosaur.
It could probably see very well with its large eyes.

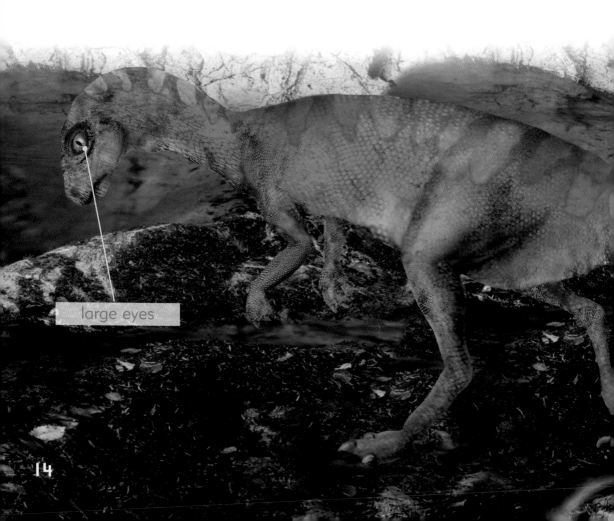

large eyes

14

Hypsilophodon could run very fast on its long legs. It held its stiff tail out to run. The tail helped the dinosaur keep its balance.

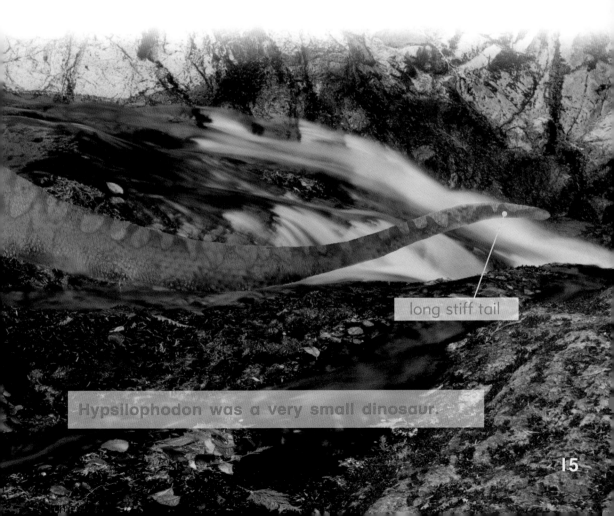

long stiff tail

Hypsilophodon was a very small dinosaur.

Hypsilophodon had teeth in the top of its hard beak, which it used to grab and tear plants. It also had cutting teeth in its cheeks. Bones dug up from the ground show us how Hypsilophodon looked.

This Hypsilophodon skeleton is a fossil made of rock.

Hypsilophodon lived in flat meadows near rivers and lakes. It lived in herds, which gave it some protection from **predator** dinosaurs.

Hypsilophodon lived in herds near lakes and rivers.

Maiasaura

(mah-ee-ah-SAWR-uh)

Maiasaura was a large dinosaur. Its hard beak was like a duck's bill. Maiasaura is called a duck-billed dinosaur.

hard beak

Maiasaura had long arms and a stiff tail. It had small bumps called **crests** in front of its eyes.

stiff tail

Maiasaura was a large dinosaur.

Maiasaura herds lived on **plains** by the sea. They used dirt and mud to build nests. The females laid about 20 eggs in each nest. When the eggs hatched, the young dinosaurs stayed in their nests.

young dinosaur

Maiasaura looked after its young in the nest. Parents fed their young and protected them from other dinosaurs. Young Maiasauras left the nest when they were bigger.

nest

Maiasaura looked after its young in the nest.

Parasaurolophus

(par-ah-SAWR-OL-uh-fus)

Parasaurolophus was a large, duck-billed dinosaur. The lower beak of the dinosaur's bill was shorter than the upper beak. Parasaurolophus used its beak to break off leaves to eat.

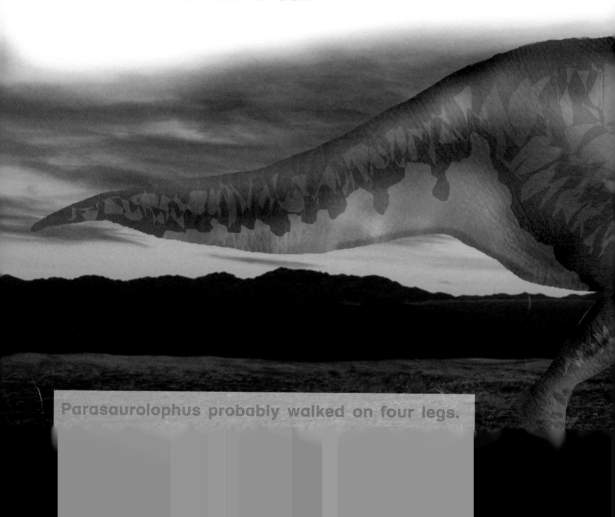

Parasaurolophus probably walked on four legs.

Parasaurolophus probably walked on four legs most of the time. It had a long crest on its head.

long crest

hard beak

The dinosaur's crest had a long **hollow** tube inside it. Parasaurolophus probably used the crest to make hooting sounds. The crest would have worked like a musical instrument.

A Parasaurolophus probably used its crest to make sounds like a trombone.

Members of Parasaurolophus families had different crests. Each kind of crest made its own sounds.

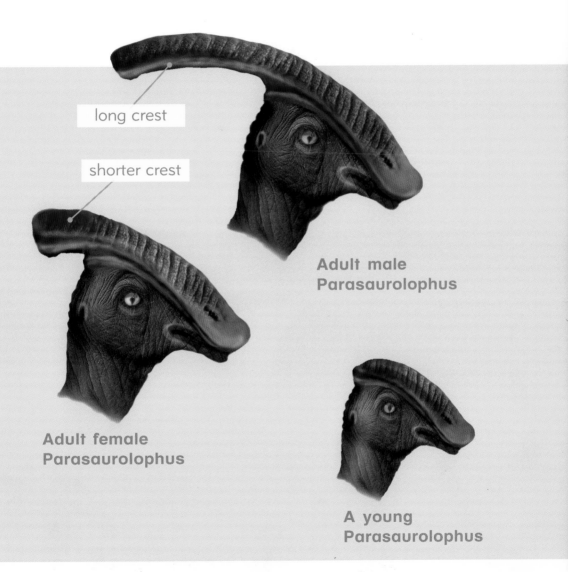

long crest

shorter crest

Adult male
Parasaurolophus

Adult female
Parasaurolophus

A young
Parasaurolophus

Corythosaurus

(ko-RITH-uh-SAWR-uhs)

Corythosaurus was a duck-billed dinosaur. It had a large, rounded crest made of bone on top of its head.

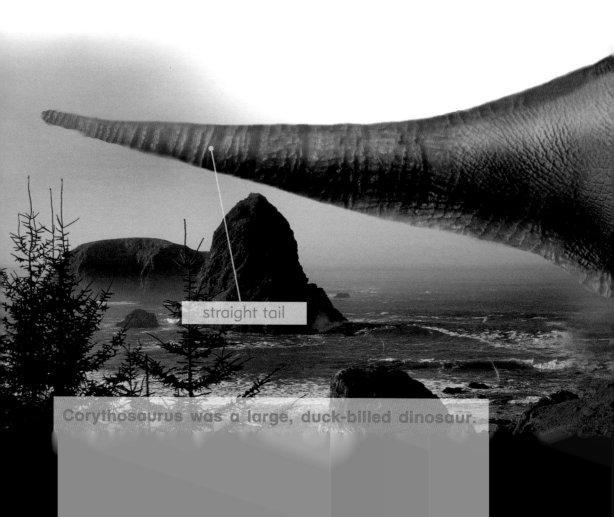

straight tail

Corythosaurus was a large, duck-billed dinosaur.

Corythosaurus had no teeth in its beak. It had many cheek teeth for grinding leaves to eat. It had a bent neck and a straight tail.

large rounded crest

bent neck

The crest of Corythosaurus had hollow tubes inside it. It was probably for making loud hooting sounds. The crests of males may have changed colour when they were looking for females.

The male Corythosaurus's crest may have changed colour when looking for females.

Corythosaurus lived on plains near the sea.
Its bones have turned into fossils and have been
dug up from the ground.

Corythosaurus skeletons have been dug up from the ground.

Names and Their Meanings

"Dinosaur" means "terrible lizard."

"Iguanodon" means "**iguana** tooth."

"Hypsilophodon" means "high-**ridge** tooth."

"Maiasaura" means "good mother lizard."

"Parasaurolophus" means "similar crested lizard."

"Corythosaurus" means "**helmet** lizard."

Glossary

crest   a ridge on an animal's body; scientists think some crests gave dinosaurs a better sense of smell or helped them make sounds.

fossil   something left behind by a plant or animal that has been preserved in the earth; examples are dinosaur bones and footprints.

helmet   a hard covering that protects the head

herd   a large group of animals that live together

hollow   to be empty inside

iguana   a type of lizard that lives today

plain   a large area of land that is mainly flat

predator   an animal that hunts other animals for food

ridge   a long raised area

skull   the bones of the head

stiff   does not bend

Index